SCHOLASTIC
News
Nonfiction Readers

Earth

by
Christine Taylor-Butler

Children's Press
An Imprint of Scholastic Inc.
New York Toronto London Auckland Sydney
Mexico City New Delhi Hong Kong
Danbury, Connecticut

These content vocabulary word builders
are for grades 1–2.

Consultant: Michelle Yehling, Astronomy Education Consultant

Photo Credits:

Photographs © 2008: Corbis Images: 4 bottom left, 4 top, 11 (Matthias Kulka), 17 (Jim Sugar); Hawaii Volcanoes National Park via SODA: 4 bottom right, 15; NASA: back cover; Peter Arnold Inc./Astrofoto: 5 bottom right, 9 top; Photo Researchers, NY: cover (European Space Agency/SPL), 1, 5 bottom left, 5 top left, 9 bottom (Mehau Kulyk); PhotoDisc/Getty Images via SODA: 2, 5 top right, 7, 23; U.S. Department of Agriculture via SODA: 19.

Illustration Credits:

Illustration page 13 by Bernard Adnet.

Illustration pages 20–21 by Greg Harris.

Book Design: Simonsays Design!
Book Production: The Design Lab

Library of Congress Cataloging-in-Publication Data
Taylor-Butler, Christine.
Earth / by Christine Taylor-Butler.—Updated ed.
  p. cm.—(Scholastic news nonfiction readers)
Includes bibliographical references and index.
ISBN-13: 978-0-531-14695-8 (lib. bdg.)   978-0-531-14760-3 (pbk.)
ISBN-10: 0-531-14695-2 (lib. bdg.)   0-531-14760-6 (pbk.)
1. Earth—Juvenile literature. I. Title.
QE501.T35 2007
550—dc22   2006102767

CONTENTS

WORD HUNT

Look for these words as you read. They will be in **bold**.

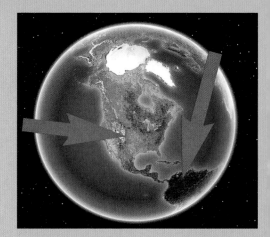

continents
(**kon**-tih-nuhnts)

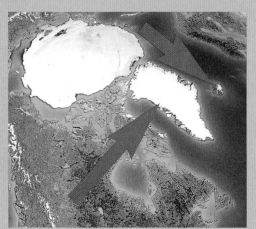

islands
(**eye**-luhndz)

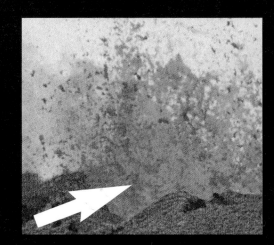

lava
(**lah**-vuh)

core
(kor)

Earth
(urth)

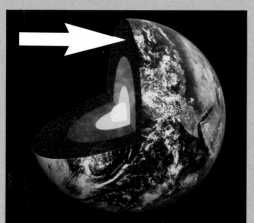

mantle
(**man**-tuhl)

solar system
(**soh**-lur **siss**-tuhm)

5

Earth!

You can eat the crust of a piece of bread.

But can you eat the crust of **Earth**?

No. Earth's crust is made of rock.

Most of Earth's crust is
covered with water.

Earth is the third planet from the Sun.

Earth is the only planet in the **solar system** with human life.

The crust is one of Earth's layers. It is the outside layer.

The **mantle** is under the crust.

The **core** is in the center of Earth.

solar system

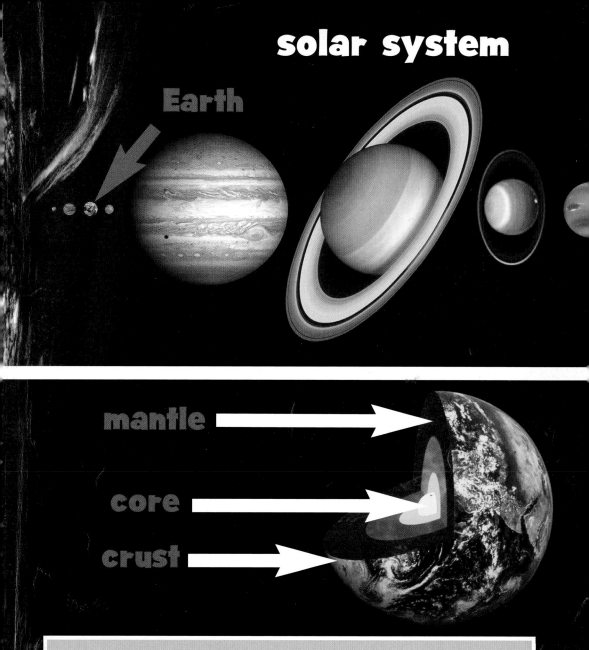

Earth

mantle

core

crust

Earth's crust is more than 40 miles
(64.5 kilometers) thick in some places.

9

Large parts of Earth's crust rise above the water.

These parts are called **continents**.

Smaller parts rise above water, too.

These parts are called **islands**.

People live on continents and islands.

island

continent

Earth has seven continents
and many islands. This
continent is North America.

Earth's crust is broken into many pieces, called plates.

These are not like dinner plates.

These plates are made of rock.

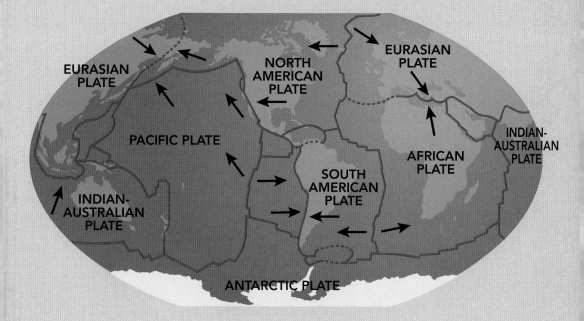

EURASIAN
PLATE

NORTH
AMERICAN
PLATE

EURASIAN
PLATE

PACIFIC PLATE

INDIAN-
AUSTRALIAN
PLATE

INDIAN-
AUSTRALIAN
PLATE

SOUTH
AMERICAN
PLATE

AFRICAN
PLATE

ANTARCTIC PLATE

The red lines show the shapes of Earth's plates.

13

Earth's mantle is under the crust.

It is made of melted rock called magma.

Earth's plates float on the magma.

Magma that comes out of Earth's crust is called **lava**.

lava

Hot lava can glow red.

Earth's plates move.

Sometimes this creates earthquakes.

Sometimes the crust pushes up.

This creates mountains.

Sometimes magma rises.

This creates a volcano.

Lava shoots out of this volcano.

We eat things that live on Earth's crust.

We eat things that grow in Earth's crust.

But we don't eat Earth's crust!

Corn is one food that grows on Earth's crust.

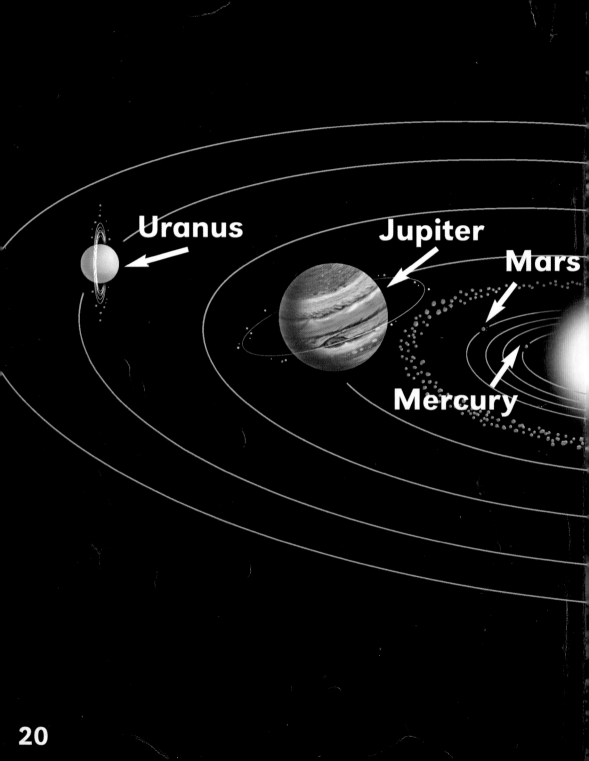

Uranus

Jupiter

Mars

Mercury

EARTH

IN OUR SOLAR SYSTEM

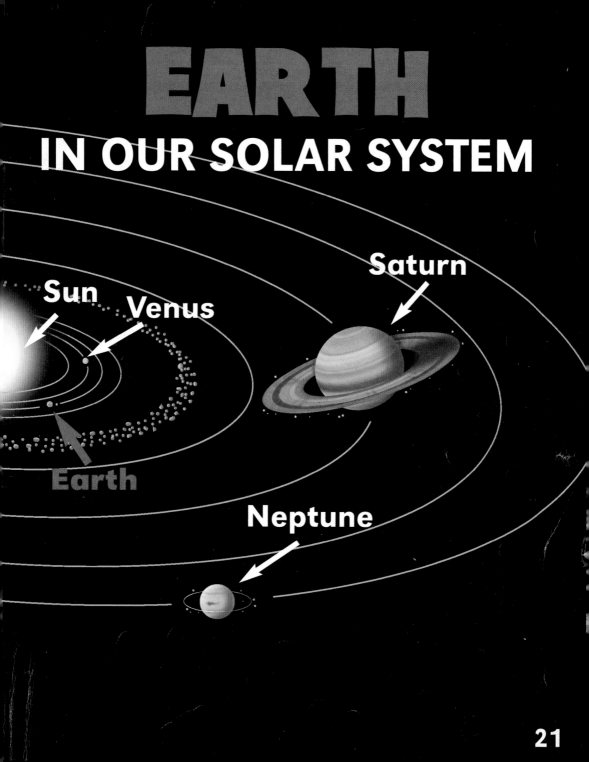

Saturn

Sun

Venus

Earth

Neptune

YOUR NEW WORDS

continents (**kon**-tih-nuhnts) very large areas of land; there are seven continents on Earth

core (kor) the center of Earth

Earth (urth) the planet we live on

islands (**eye**-luhndz) small areas of land that rise above the water

lava (**lah**-vuh) hot magma that comes out of a volcano

mantle (**man**-tuhl) the layer between Earth's crust and the core

solar system (**soh**-lur **siss**-tuhm) the group of planets, moons, and other things that travel around the Sun

Earth Is an Amazing Planet!

 A year is how long it takes a planet to go around the Sun.
1 Earth year=365 days

 A day is how long it takes a planet to turn one time.
1 Earth day = 24 hours

Earth has 1 moon.

Earth is more than 4 billion years old.

Earth is the only planet in the solar system with liquid water on its surface.

INDEX

FIND OUT MORE

Book:

Luhr, James F., ed. *Smithsonian Earth*. New York: DK Publishing, Inc., 2003.

Web site:

Solar System Exploration
http://sse.jpl.nasa.gov/planets

MEET THE AUTHOR

Christine Taylor-Butler is the author of more than twenty books for children. She holds a degree in Engineering from M.I.T. She lives in Kansas City with her family where they have a telescope for searching the skies.